YOU ARE A RAINBOW

YOU ARE

ESSENTIAL

A

AURAS

RAINBOW

EMMA LUCY KNOWLES

POP PRESS

Published in 2020 by Pop Press an imprint of Ebury Publishing,
20 Vauxhall Bridge Road, London SW1V 2SA

Pop Press is part of the Penguin Random House group of companies
whose addresses can be found at global.penguinrandomhouse.com

Penguin
Random House
UK

First published by Pop Press in 2020

www.penguin.co.uk

A CIP catalogue record for this book is available from the British Library

ISBN 9781529107272

Design by Imagist

Typeset in 9/12 pt Neuzeit Office Pro
by Integra Software Services Pvt. Ltd, Pondicherry

Printed and bound in Great Britain by Clays Ltd, Elcograf S.p.A.

MIX
Paper from
responsible sources
FSC
www.fsc.org   FSC® C018179

Penguin Random House is committed to a sustainable future for
our business, our readers and our planet. This book is made from
Forest Stewardship Council® certified paper.

Contents

Introducing the Power of Auras

You are a beautiful mass of rainbow-coloured, high-vibing, far-flowing energy, vibrating and emitting your own unique frequency out into the world and even out into the universe – think of yourself as a magical unicorn, if you will! This frequency, these vibrations, these *vibes*, are an energetical extension of yourself – a collaborative force that is lovingly named and known as your aura.

Now, your aura is full of endless opportunities and potential. It's your personal landscape and it's just waiting for you to tune in and lean into it, so that you can tap in to your own energy waves and your own frequency, which in turn will allow you to radiate as the super beam you truly are. I want to work with you to attract what you truly deserve and live the high-vibe life that we all crave but which can often feel unobtainable. The world of today is one in which the spiritual and the material realms have collided, causing conflict and strain, yes, and inner battles too, but which has ultimately moved us into a new wave of growth. We are learning, unlearning and re-learning what is good or right for us, breaking through the old materialistic thinking of 'we get what we deserve' and investing in spiritual practices that allow us to grow on a deeper level – emotionally and physically – and tap into a flow that is so much more encompassing than we have previously been taught or known: welcome to the Now Age!

What You will Discover in Your Aura – and this Book

The frequency of your aura – your frequency – is super-important because your aura is like a welcome sign to who you are. It introduces you even before your voice does, because where you are at emotionally, mentally, physically, spiritually, and your beliefs radiate through its energy. And it works both ways – it's also how you make your initial, lightning-bolt appraisal of a fellow human being ... as they do of you.

You know when you walk into a room or a bar and you instinctively know who you want to walk towards, who makes you feel safe? Who you 'like', who you don't and who you want to walk away from? You'll recognise that intuitive knowing that bristles in your being – it's like shivers, tingles or a mild electric shock! That happens because your aura is calling out across the room as you enter it, sending out a signal, a transmission that broadcasts your unique frequency, like your own innate Wi-Fi hotspot that you have cleverly, subconsciously created. And your frequency is just like a magnet calling out to 'its kind' or 'its people' – those who resonate with you, who are vibing at the same pace or frequency as you, either overall or on one of the levels within your auric field.

The opposite is also true. The more aware you are of your energy, the quicker the red flags will tickle you when someone or something is off ... and when you need to investigate this. Often we let other people into our lives or our energies, only to realise after months have passed that their vibe is not right for us and we then have to set about unpicking the situation, which, by this stage, is much harder work. By applying daily or weekly check-ins with your energy, you are being incredibly responsible both for yourself and others, and taking care of yourself on a whole other level, using your energy to work with love to strengthen or indeed release relationships, habits and ways of thinking that no longer suit or serve you before they sink in deep. Remember, always start with yourself – your vibe attracts your tribe, after all. Your frequency will magnetise what appeals to its auric shade, so first and foremost you need to check in and see where your energy and aura are at and what you can change within yourself to release the painful or the now unwanted energies, and instead attract the right energies and people who will help you to shine and fulfil your potential.

Understand Your Power and Potential

By opening this book, you are rather excitingly committing to opening up and outwards towards the expansive layers of your self – those layers that usually remain unseen but which are most definitely felt! To learn (with fun!) and understand more about who YOU truly are, the power and potential of this, and, what is more, the power you possess to shape your own life right here, right now, and also a little further up the road ahead, into your future – as well as coming to understand the impact you have on others and their life and days.

In this book, you will learn what your aura is, what it is made of and therefore what *you* are made of; how the aura works and as a result how you work; and how to take back your power by simply feeling for it. How to honour your light, your vibes – your aura – and then really start to feel your way into understanding how what you put out into the world energetically, above and beyond your words and your beautiful face, is why you get back from it what you do (both positive and negative). I am going to show you how to feel, influence, cleanse, heal, recharge and realign your aura and your energy field with some vibing exercises and energetic practices. (Yes, you will have to do some work, but it won't be like PE and it will be so worth it!)

Your aura is just like your physical body in that your body is built up of a network of organs, blood cells, chemical reactions and so on, coming together to form the miraculous shape of you. Your aura is the same, only it's the embodiment of all your wondrous energetical networks. It's the energetical mirror, reflection and expansion of all the energy that expands from everything that you are made up of within – your bones and organs, yes, but also the energy of your mood, your thoughts and your emotions. Each and all of these has a frequency of energy or a *vibe* that they emit, and these vibes dance together to form the shape, quality and texture of the whole picture, which is beautifully named your aura.

Brighten Your Aura and Open Your World

The quality of your energy is super-important, and embracing and understanding your aura will allow you to generate more energy and brightness, making you quite literally feel more alive and more able to power through your work or to find a new job more in tune with your vibe. It will allow you to connect with your tribe, your people, support you in making the choices that will lead you to your dreams and destiny, and be healthier in body and spirit. Your auric energy will also help you to sink into a deeper sleep – ok, it may not be able to eradicate all the problems in life as they are part of the learning, but it will allow you to face into them with a degree of peacefulness and calm control.

You will learn how to cleanse your aura and heal your energies, where you may previously have not healed or been loving or deserving of your beautiful self, and where your self-worth may be in need of some TLC. Perhaps you have let another person plant a negative seed in your mind, who in turn has invited you to grow it as yours? Knowing your aura means knowing and harnessing your energies, and tuning into your vibe so you know what is yours and what is someone else's. If a seed has been planted and you are fussing over it, overanalysing it and pondering over your belief in it – then now is the time to heal it, free it, release it from your aura and truly let it go. Change the situation and the energy in your aura, for your energy is too rich, too precious to be allowed to leak out on the undeserving, the unwilling and the unnecessary.

Some of us walk around completely obliviously, with an energy hangover, simply accepting our situation is our lot in life – but it is *not*! Opening your mind to your full potential on a spiritual or energetical level has life-changing benefits and your aura is a huge part of that. From my own personal experience and the energy work I do with many an amazing human being, I've seen first-hand how by just scratching the surface of working with your energy and your aura – and even just acknowledging that it can have huge positive changes on your life, your mindset, and how you see yourself and how others see you – what felt like 'blocks' in life can fade away. Those 'blocks' were merely part of a belief system that has been lingering, uninvited, within our energy flow.

We are all so much more than we dare to dream, dare to allow, dare to believe and dare to *see*, and as we come to learn how to plant our feet all the more firmly and deeply in the Now Age, we can make our own lives and the world a whole lot brighter.

So this book is dedicated to the light that you are, the light that you perhaps don't yet know, and the light and colour that you bring to the world, and to each and every person or being you pass and touch every day without even knowing it. Thank you for your You-ness!

What is an Aura?

The question 'what is an aura?' could also be expressed as 'who are you and what are you really made of?'

If you're interested enough to be reading this book (and thank you!), you've most definitely heard of an aura or have an understating of what that means to you, but perhaps you haven't swum in its depths as much as you'd like to – so let's dive in.

Let's start with what you can see of yourself in the mirror: you can see your physical body, the physical marks of life upon that beautiful body and, as you look into your face, deep into your eyes (not that that's particularly comfortable!), you can see the happiness or perhaps the worry that may be dancing upon your expression right now. You can feel, touch and scrutinise these aspects of yourself with your five senses and you can love or hurt (depending, as always, on your mood or experience) these parts of yourself with your words and either unlimited or limited self-care.

Our aura is our energy mirror, reflecting back to us our state of being, our emotional and energetic state. Just as we all have an aura, so too do we all have the ability to 'see' it and to cleanse, recharge and realign it. And just as we are all unique, individual human beings, so we all have unique, individual and different ways of working with and therefore 'seeing' our auras. With time, practice and a healthy dose of patience, we can learn to 'see' our brilliance in all its glory and trust in it, just as we do in the invisible power of the Wi-Fi connection at home or in a coffee shop.

What's in a Name?

Quite a lot actually ...

The word 'aura' is of Latin origin and means, quite beautifully, 'wind', 'breath of air' or 'breeze'. In Greek mythology, Aura was the daughter of a Titan, goddess of the breeze and the fresh, cool air of early morning ... How blissful and peaceful is that?

More commonly, aura is a word used to describe the atmosphere or a 'quality' that is generated by and which in turn surrounds each and every human being, thing or place. From my point of view and, yes, that's a spiritual one, an aura is so much more than simply a descriptive term for what we or a place or an object gives off. It is a completely crucial part of who we are; it is our own energy universe, which is layered with emotional, mental and spiritual brilliance, and which doesn't just surround the body but is emitted *from* our physical body. It's our 'Bat-Signal' out into life, our own personal Wi-Fi, if you will, that enables us to seek out what we want and need.

When we align ourselves with our aura, set our frequency and come into contact with someone whose aura and energy is clear, cool and radiating on a level that resonates with our own aura, it can feel to us, as the Latin term suggests, as if they are quite literally an energetical breath of fresh air: they lift our spirits as though they were the wind beneath our wings. Dreamy!

Your Own Universe

Let's compare ourselves for a minute to a mega ball of energy – the Earth. Visualise the Earth and consider her multiple layers: on the surface alone, there are all those living organisms feeding off her brilliance; before moving deep down towards her core, layer upon layer, depth upon depth, each with a purpose that allows the Earth to grow and spin and do mind-blowing, phenomenal things ... We can resonate with that level of depth, can't we? As human beings, we too are wonderful beings of energy who, under the surface, under the skin, are home to an incredible ecosystem, providing layer upon layer of brilliance within ourselves that keep us alive without thought ...

But what holds the Earth? What supports her? Gravity holds her, the ozone layer protects her. And then there is this huge expanse of universe, this energy that goes on beyond measure, in which the Earth plays an important part – a universe whose intricacies we are only just starting to understand. So would it really be too crazy to allow yourself to consider that just as we go as deep as the Earth, so we too radiate out a whole lot more than we completely realise or understand at present, just as she does? And that just as the Earth and each planet and moon and star within our solar system plays a unique and crucial role in our universe's survival, so we too – as individuals – do the same thing down here on Earth? That we are each of us playing a unique yet important role that we don't quite as yet entirely understand, radiating and expanding beyond (energetically) where our human eyes allow us to perceive, into our own energy universe? A universe of the self that in turns reaches out and touches the energy universe of each and every other being on the planet? An energy universe that is known as our aura.

Auras in Time, Science and Art

As with all things energy, I am pleased to report that we cannot track or exactly pinpoint when auras came into our lives, because they didn't – they have always been there. We are born with them: they are 100 per cent part of the beautifulness that is being human and there is even some scientific research and recognition to support this. In fact, science has been actively investigating our energy bodies since the early 1800s! Although they do not name it as we might, scientists have noted a 'subtle body' of energy, an energy field or human electromagnetic field, which is classed as being far too delicate to fully analyse, but which exists around all living things. They have therefore concluded that all living beings transmit energy, sending out a vibration and frequency.

In fact, this body of energy, your aura, has been the subject of much scientific fascination. There are several notable names in the realm of human energy investigations across the ages – we will give a nod to three. First up is Baron Dr Carl Ludwig von Reichenbach, whose research in the nineteenth century concluded that several properties unique to our human energy field are shared with natural atmospheric or man-made electromagnetic fields. (Think of the build-up of charge in the atmosphere that comes with a thunderstorm or the vibe you can see buzzing around pylon cables!) In the human form, Reichenbach called this 'the Odic force', later renaming it 'the subtle body', but where science concluded that opposites attract within electromagnetic fields, he noted that in our energy body, like attracts like.

Next we have Dr Walter J Kilner, who in the early twentieth century took to some very special experimental practices in his research of human energy, exploring it through coloured filters and a special mix of coal tar! He discovered we have three 'zones' in our energy body: a dark layer next to the skin, a more ethereal layer flowing off the body at an angle and also a very delicate exterior layer. He concluded (most importantly) that the state of this 'aura' (yes, that's what he called it) changed in reaction to a subject's state of mind and their health.
 A few years later, Dr Wilhelm Reich furthered our knowledge and understanding of the human energy field when he noted that areas of 'congestion' within the human energy field could be 'cleared' to release negative mental and emotional patterns and effect change within our mind and body.

You will also recognise the concept of auras in many forms of art, religion and popular culture. Our bodies of light, our auras, have been 'seen', felt and witnessed through artistic mediums right across the ages – auras aren't just figments of our imaginations. In art, we can see halos of light around angels and the enlightened beings that adorn temples and churches, and they are also mentioned in many sacred scriptures. These bodies of light have been ever-present in religion across the ages, from Hinduism and Buddhism, from the thinking that the colour of our aura is intrinsically linked to Kundalini energy and our chakras, right through to the Christian and Islamic faiths and their beliefs in light sources and bodies of light. Humans have always recognised that we have this energetic layer surrounding us; we've just – as with most things – changed and reshaped the name, or established varying beliefs as to what an aura is.

As we will come to see shortly, our aura is made of vibes, but it is also layered like a cake! It has seven layers, to be precise. A belief that energy is expressed in seven layers that affect our health is shared across many ancient medicine systems, some of which remain familiar to us today, such as Ayurveda and the chakra system.

In this Now Age, we've seen a re-emergence of the original call for 'no bad vibes' or 'good vibes only' that started to appear in the swinging sixties with the Flower Power movement. A standout moment for me, it was when Rhianna sang about incredible auras in 'Don't Stop the Music'. At the age of thirteen, I was happily telling my sister to 'back out my aura' (without knowing what on Earth it was). Here, as we delve deeper into the significance of the aura, you should know that your own personal interpretation will be crucial in how you use and work with your knowledge and energy – and therefore your aura.

How do Auras work?

As mentioned, our aura consists of seven layers, which are also known as planes – so you can think of your aura as being like a rainbow of energy: it is equally colourful! Each layer of your aura has a system of connections that links it to specific aspects of your mind, body and spiritual being. Its energy is governed by the experiences, knowledge, feelings and thoughts that are driven by those parts of your being. One layer of your aura, for example, is associated with health, another with emotions, and the next with your ego and your beliefs. We will explore each of these layers in more depth in the next chapter. It is also important to be aware that what you think, believe, feel and speak, and how fit and healthy you are, all have a direct effect on the quality of your energy and your vibe within each layer of your aura – and also its colour. (More on that to come too!)

These layers of energy, vibrating together collaboratively and collectively, form your aura and blend to create your own unique energy tone and frequency, which becomes your very own 'Bat-Signal' – the make-up of the frequency that you send out into the world and which, as a result, governs what you attract back, based on the level of that vibration.

The Language of Colours

Our aura is very cleverly colour-coded – I told you to think unicorns and rainbows, didn't I? Each layer has a colour (or colours) that sings of where you are at in your life right now, be that emotionally, physically or mentally. You are awash with colour, although some colours may be more dominant than others (think of a tie-dye T-shirt), which is why they are easier to see or more present at your time of viewing them. Esoteric studies have aligned these colours to an energy language, in which each colour relates to who you are and where you are at in life, allowing you to radiate and realise your greatest potential. I believe that we each have our own unique interpretation of the colours and we will therefore be exploring colour themes, as well as investigating your unique colour-code and how you can influence the colour of your aura's vibe.

Before we start looking at your aura and each delicate yet powerful layer, it's important to know why and how you will benefit from 'knowing' them at a deeper level. And it's all good news – because you have the ability to monitor, change and manage your energy and therefore your aura. If you know that you are allergic or intolerant to some foods, you stop eating them, right? You wean them out of your diet and replace them with a healthier alternative. It's the same with your aura and its energy make-up: thinking cruelly about yourself impacts the frequency of the energy (and the crueller the thought, the lower the vibe), but the more positive and affirming the thought, the higher the vibe – it's that simple. This means that a single thought pattern can rock your whole energy network and the signal you are sending out to the world and therefore what you attract back. By being able to read and understand your aura, you can see what is affecting it or where you can add more light and shine, what needs to change or transform, and so just as you would swap out foods from your diet, by taking out what doesn't agree with you, you can also alter or emotionally heal your energy to up your vibe.

Like Attracts Like

Our aura is very clever and just like a two-way radio, it calls and receives – and it does one better than that – it gives! Our aura and the energies within it reacts to the energy and auras of others on many levels, so it's important to know energetically who we are really interacting with, as some people's energy can calm us or energise us, while others may leave us feeling a little flat or deflated. Once we understand our aura's reaction to someone else's energy, we can learn how to protect ourselves from someone who is draining us and learn how to draw in those who charge us up. This is the key to your auric health as well of that of your mind, body and spirit.

Most importantly, when it comes to energy, always remember that 'like attracts like'. This is why we are going to explore how to honour your aura and your energy: how to clear it, cleanse it, heighten it and set your signal or your frequency to attract an energetically healthy, high-vibe tribe of friends, to attract or improve your relationships, lift your mood, focus your mindset, let yourself flow where you have been unknowingly stagnant, make every day brighter, improve your health, attract a new job or make the current one more in keeping with your flow.

But it's also very important to note that just as we should never judge a book by its cover, nor should we judge anyone by their energy. We are not the same person from one day to the next, as our experience on any given day or time can unexpectedly shape our mood and therefore our energy. Just as you can change your energy, so can others; so rather than using your knowledge as an excuse not to like someone or to judge them because they're not on your 'level' energetically speaking, use your insights as a tool for creating compassion for them and yourself. Work instead towards understanding their energy (i.e. why they are like that, or what in your own energy is leaning away from them and why) and ask how you can interact with them without having to change your own vibe or seeking to change theirs. Understanding and exploring, rather than controlling or avoiding these energetic relationships, will help you with everyone you interact with – work colleagues, neighbours, strangers, even your friends and family.

There is no 'off' switch for your aura, but you can always vibe up or vibe down the energy in it. You can raise and expand your vibe so that your aura can really be 'seen', or dial it back in order to keep a low profile. It's a two-way radio, remember, and we will look at how to vibe up and radiate outwards, or keep a low profile and reset your auric vibe messaging, depending on where you feel you need to be.

Rainbow Waves: The Structure of Your Aura

Tap into your own energy waves and radiate as the super-beam you truly are.

As touched upon earlier, our aura is made up of seven energetical layers which provide a live feed of how and where we are emotionally and energetically on a day-to-day basis, with each layer telling its own unique tale. Our aura acts like a little like an eggshell or the ozone layer of the Earth. It encloses our body all over – back, front, centre, above and below and all things in-between – and it connects in and out and to all things in-between!

Like our physical body, our energetical or spiritual body is a complex being. It's time now to introduce chakras to you in more detail. You probably have some awareness of chakras, but the important thing here is that although chakras form a separate system, there is a powerful link between our auric layers and the major chakras, and they have an effect on each other. Your chakras are vortexes of powerful energy and they are internal, residing within your body. The colours of the chakras remain constant throughout your life (unless you experience a major life-changing event). Your aura, however, is an external force and the colour of your aura (both its layers and as a whole) varies with your mood, emotions and experiences each day. As you change over time, so does your aura – its nature is not set in stone at birth.

Not only is the colour of your aura influenced by your physical, emotional and spiritual health, the size of your aura is also influenced by these factors. When these factors are balanced and healthy, your aura can stretch out far and wide; when out of balance, your mind and body can feel heavy and 'small' – that's your energy moving inwards, as your aura retreats from the outside world. Exercises and practices later in this book will help you to explore which layer you want to work on to cleanse and heighten the impact of your aura, but first it's time to see what governs each layer.

Your Auric Layers

Let's take a closer look at the aura, layer by layer, as the first step towards understanding it before moving on to seeing or sensing your own aura and working with it.

LAYER 1 – THE ETHERIC BODY OR PHYSICAL AURA PLANE (OUR HEALTH)

This is the layer of the aura that lies closest to our physical body, so it's also the easiest of the auric layers to see with ye old human eye. It bears witness to the effects of our health (mainly physical but also our emotional health), both our pleasures and our pains. If you feel full of vitality, energised and ready to go, or, alternatively, if you pull a muscle, have a cold or cut your finger, this will be shown and take effect in this layer. If you are injured, this is a great layer for you to focus on, as we can use the energy in this layer to aid a speedy recovery and to nurture the body as it heals.

Sleep, rest and relaxation really affect this layer – they increase its vitality. The Etheric Body diminishes in vibrancy throughout the day, much like your phone battery does until you plug it in and charge it back up. Similarly, your Etheric Body is fuelled by rest and recovery. It is associated also with the root or base chakra – that feeling and energy of being really connected to life and to who we are on this Earth.

Athletes, dancers and general high-frequency movers live in this layer of the aura. They are able to conserve and then give off a punch of the high energy held in this strengthening layer at just the right time. But while rest recharges this layer, the more sedentary you are, the weaker your etheric layer tends to be. The good news is, however, that this layer is not just empowered by being a health junkie; physical comfort (so, yes, cuddles and baths!) and other pleasures alongside general good health also bring greater strength and balance.

It is super-important to know that it is a layer affected by negative emotions and harsh environments. Whether you are harbouring, thinking or witnessing them, dwelling in hard, harsh and negative emotions has real impact on this layer. Of course, life isn't always easy and we know that sometimes situations are beyond our control – and that negative thoughts and patterns tend to recycle themselves – so you will find meditations, exercises and quick hits later in this book that will allow you to top up this layer, even when your current situation doesn't feel that it is fuelling or empowering you.

Focus on this layer: when you need an energy hit or when you feel depleted in vitality or health.

LAYER 2 – THE EMOTIONAL BODY OR ASTRAL AURA PLANE (OUR EMOTIONAL LIBRARY)

Layer 2 does exactly what it says on the box – it's the layer of our emotions! This is what I like to call the 'emotional library layer', where our emotional history and experiences (both good and bad) are conveniently stored for recall and use whenever we should need them. The Emotional Body has a strong association with the sacral chakra or energy centre that governs our emotions, so it can represent self-empowerment or self-flagellation, depending on what's on your emotional shelves. This means it is all the more important to heal, forgive and let go, as holding on to negative emotion or burying situations and experiences that caused you pain will only take up energetical space that you really don't need to give to them for one moment longer. It's time to delete files in this library, clear your mental browsing history and free up your energy storage for more positive intention. Healing on this layer will also allow you to soothe, witness and, over time, lessen the triggers that have emotionally held you prisoner for far too long.

We can tell when our Emotional Body is out of whack because we feel it: we can become sensitive, hypercritical and vulnerable for seemingly no reason, and irrational and short-tempered with those we love. We can also become picky, pokey, lacking in trust and looking for proof when we ought to be looking for love.

The Emotional Body responds to its surroundings, so you will know if you are in the right room with the right people by how you feel. It's also the layer that interacts the most with another's and we will explore later how to separate energetically what is yours from what belongs to someone else – gently and with love.

To best lift the energy of this layer, get outside or change your surroundings. Stuck in a fight? Open the windows at home, let in the fresh air and move. Where that is not possible, then stop, take stock and take a breath. Visualise the colour green or take a crystal that is green in colouring (aventurine, amazonite, jade are my starting suggestions for you here). Green is the colour of nature but green is also the colour of the heart chakra and a soothing colour for this emotional layer.

Focus on this layer: when you are feeling locked in conflict, seek to let go and forgive, or aim to feel all the more by opening your heart.

LAYER 3 – THE MENTAL BODY OR LOWER MENTAL AURA PLANE (OUR BELIEF PATTERNS)

'What you believe you become. Your thoughts become things.' So the old adage goes and nothing could be truer when said of layer 3, aka your Mental Body. This is the layer of the auric self that resonates and responds to our old pal, the ego. Our ego is that part of us that believes it is keeping us 'safe' when actually it is keeping us small. It's the voice in our mind that tells us that we couldn't possibly do that, or questions why anyone would like us or why we deserve the treatment that we've received. This layer is usually the elaborate construction of your values and your beliefs, be that about the world, life, others, and, most importantly, your thoughts about yourself.

All these beliefs, values and patterns come together to create your everyday reality and therefore the energy lens through which you perceive the world and your place within it. Like a balloon, good patterns and beliefs can inflate this layer – they become the breath that fills it. However, sometimes those beliefs are not so constructive and they deflate and deplete this layer.

However, our energy does not lie and it acts as an alarm for when we have got stuck in a rut or are in a pattern that we might not yet have consciously realised is bringing us down. If we are tuned into this energy, we can raise the roof of the vibration, reset the frequency and realign ourselves to a more uplifting state of being. Later in the book, we will work towards healing and soothing the beliefs that cause us harm.

The Mental Body is also where we spend most of our energetical time throughout the day when we are working, learning and studying. If we are in a focused state, we are mainly held within this energy space and this layer expands and is fuelled when our mind is engaged or focused on something (even if it's golf). It's also the layer associated with the almighty solar plexus chakra, the centre of our personal power. We need this layer to be fit and healthy in order to keep moving forward in life, so it's super-important that we keep working on our beliefs about ourselves and kick out anything from our energy and mind that says we can't. Positive, powerful energy and self-belief will always win out over our ego's attempts to diminish us.

When we are feeling out of whack, we can feel judged, humiliated, embarrassed, down, flat or agitated. This acts as a red flag that we need to spend some time inflating this layer with kind and happy talk about ourselves – both with ourselves and with other people.

Focus on this layer: when you need to commit to or concentrate on a project or task and to promote a positive perception of yourself.

LAYER 4 - THE ASTRAL BODY OR HIGHER MENTAL AURA PLANE (WHERE OUR HEART IS)

If we were to split the aura neatly into two halves, we would say that layer 4, the Astral Body, is the space between all those qualities that relate to our being human and all those aspects that allow us to be spiritual. It's the layer that connects and communicates all things other worldly with the Mental Body but from a deeper, more spiritual stance. It's also the layer associated with and connected to the heart – and to the heart chakra, the queen of the energy centres. When we talk about listening to our gut or trusting our instincts, this is the auric layer that does this.

This level of our aura vibrates with those higher mental beliefs. This is where we hold and store a frequency of self-love, unconditional gratitude and selflessness. It's where we hold our feelings about the bigger picture – the world as a whole and the universe – and it's therefore the layer at which we hold those beliefs that allows us to connect energetically with 'like-minded' folk, who hold the same visions and values as ourselves. An abundance of self-love, gratitude and selflessness allow us to generate confidence in our true self-identity and to project this out energetically into the world.

Self-talk will really affect your signal here, so whenever you look in the mirror and think negatively of yourself, know you are draining this pot. Others may also throw words at you in anger or cruelty but don't let their harsh vibes or misjudged beliefs take up one second of your light. This is a layer that is really affected when we're in an emotional break-up or if we feel like we are losing our grip on something or someone we have held dear and as a result feel emotionally down and out. If that's a space you find yourself in right now, we can work at this layer in the chapter 'Taking Care of Your Aura'.

Focus on this layer: when you want to attract your people, your tribe, for a greater love of self and others and to heal your heart's aches and pains!

LAYER 5 – THE ETHERIC TEMPLATE OR SPIRITUAL AURA PLANE (SPEAKING OUT)

Layer 5 is where things get all the more magical – for this is your manifestation layer, which allows you to call out for and attract into your life that which you desire, which is why it has strong associations with the throat chakra energy centre. It is incredibly multi-layered because its vibe is a reflection of our spiritual health and our connection to our immediate surroundings, as well as to the wider universe. The energy within this layer is a true representation of our personality and our overall energy – a blueprint, as it were, for our entire identity.

When we are aware of and working in this layer, we can really connect to other people's spiritual plane – like that feeling when you have met someone for only five minutes, but it feels like five years, or if you have a dear friend you see once in a blue moon, but you pick straight back up where you started energetically and positively – even though six months or six years have passed. People who are flowing at you freely in this layer can feel even closer than family; it's a super-special place in which to connect, but – and this is a huge but – not everyone swims in this plane. We all have the capability to do so, but some people are set to what I call 'human' mode – a safe space that allows them to remain 'inside the box' and so to step outside of their beliefs feels to them (or, I would say, 'fears' to them) to be a near impossible state to reach, even if deep down they would love to.

When this layer is out of sorts, we can perceive it through our emotions once more and this is echoed in our words. We become cynical and judgemental both towards ourselves and others. We can almost feel threatened and backed into a corner, and stunted within our spiritual growth. These are our tells and we can use them to lift and shift the vibe. Expression is key here as the Etheric Template is associated with our throat chakra, remember, so scream, shout, paint, dance, express yourself – *let it all out*!

Focus on this layer: when you are looking to connect on a higher level, to clear away jealousy or hurt caused by another, to soothe your emotions and speak your truth.

LAYER 6 – THE CELESTIAL BODY OR INTUITIONAL AURA PLANE (DIVINING OUR DREAMS)

Our celestial body, layer 6 in our aura, is one of my favourites – for it is one that allows us to go beyond ourselves, our beliefs and our limitations into a space of heightened spiritual awareness, a place full of knowing and filled with those sweet 'ah ha' intuitive moments. It's about flowing along, at ease with life rather than forcing it. It's also my favourite because it's where we store our dreams – dreams for growth and adventure, love and romance. It's the layer that allows you to hand these dreams over to the universe for their manifestation in the real world. And it's the sweet spot for tapping into and flowing wider with our intuition, so has strong connections with our third eye, the chakra that allows us to 'see' intuitively.

When this layer is in balance, we experience a greater sense of spiritual awareness. It is a place where we can energetically believe in all those things that are unseen yet almighty in their power. Working with our energy here can allow us to lean into the magic of the universe without human worry blocking our path; we tap into our raw manifestation power, taking what we communicated in layer 5 and expanding that even further spiritually.

It's also a space where we store forgiveness and acceptance – our true nature of peace, patience and calm that allows us to forgive, accept and trust. It empowers us, allows us to feel 'safe' and most importantly shows us how to be kind.

We can truly sense people who have worked in this layer, as being in their presence allows us to feel safe, held and connected to life beyond our front door without knowing why. We can sense when our vibe is off in this layer as we will feel stuffy, almost lacking in creativity, as though nothing 'new' is coming nor possible. It's important to clear our viewpoint so we can trust our spiritual sight and access our intuitive voice.

Focus on this layer: when looking to manifest your dreams, heighten your intuition, connect with your spirit and the universe.

LAYER 7 – THE CAUSAL PLANE OR ABSOLUTE AURA PLANE

Layer 7 is also known as the Causal Plane (relating to our soul and our spiritual balance), but I like to call it the 'veil'. It is the Causal Plane, our own personal seventh heaven and the layer of our aura that is filled with our purest potential. This is the layer that connects you to the divine, however you come to know or believe in it, and it is also the layer that seeks to balance and soothe all the other layers within your aura. This layer hones the blueprint of your soul. It's like a supercomputer for all the experiences of your soul's journey – including those past-life experiences that your soul seeks to soothe or for which you are honoured with the knowledge gained across these lifetimes of travel. The highest-vibing of all the layers, the Causal Layer is our energy lifeline to our divine connection and it is linked beautifully with our crown chakra, the energy centre at the top of our head that connects us to the higher power.

We can tell when this layer is off-kilter as we may feel squashed or we do not enjoy being in our body. Our thoughts are on loop rather than free-flowing, and rather than being open-minded and expansive, we cannot see the wood for the trees.

Focus on this layer: when you are seeking balance, clarity and a greater sense of knowing and being.

Commit to your vibe, your frequency, and just watch how powerfully the universe waves back at you.

A Rainbow of Colours: What Your Aura is Saying

You are a colour-coded, high-vibing energy beacon of multi-tonal radiant light!

Eighties singer Cyndi Lauper saw your true colours shining through – they were beautiful like a rainbow, she sang, and she's right, you know!

As you work on your aura, you will start to 'see' different colours starting to show themselves to you through each layer and how there are varying tones of these colours on different days! Each colour has a meaning, a message if you like. Each colour is an honest reflection of where you are at emotionally, physically and mentally. In seeing and knowing the meaning of each colour, you can get a true sense of where you stand in life, remembering always that your energy changes by the day and that sometimes you may feel weakened due to poor mental habits or the low-vibe quality of the people and surroundings you find yourself among. Remember, this is not a fixed state of being and you can lift and expand those colours and the vibes they swim along to their full vibrancy!

The first thing to know is that the brightness of a colour – the vibrancy and clarity of it – holds meaning and it's this brightness that we look for: a deep shade of navy with a brightness to it is a rich energy to behold, while a deep red is similarly powerful, so look for this quality in the colours you see. The colours can, however, look and feel dull, cloudy, lacking in vibrancy and lustre, but if you feel a little dull in your light or vibe, know that you are not stuck there: it's more of a spiritual or energetical flash card, a call to attention for you to invoke and invite change where you may have been hiding your truth away before!

Remember, there is no specific colour for each layer. Your aura is made up of a wash of colour and as with a rainbow, the closer you get to it the more you can see the colours merging and blurring. Some colours and therefore their associations will be clearer or louder than others, depending on what you need to be witnessing within yourself right now.

RED FOR STRENGTH (SUB-COLOUR PINK)

Red is as punchy a colour as we know it to be. It is a powerful indicator of the physical layer and your physical body and health. To see a bright, clear, crisp, delicious hue of red in your aura represents strength – strength of your energy, of body and of character! What's more, it signals that you and your energy are realistic and well grounded; in this day and age, that deserves a 'well done you'!

Red auric energy signifies an active, energetic being, a creative person filled with the potential of life and a love for it. Dancing in red rays shows you are in a determined, courageous state of being, bathing in vitality, sexual power and passion.

SUB-COLOUR PINK

On a softer front, a red that is moving into fluffy pink suggests that you are heart-led and open, generous with your affections, and ready, willing and open to receive affection at the same measure with which you give. When red moves to pink, it sings of happiness and talks to the empath, the healthy fantasist and the magic-maker who does all things passionately and who bubbles in – you guessed it – love.

WHEN IN SHADE

The duller or the cloudier the colour, the more your energy is expressing a need to release anger and irritation. These muted shades of red are an alert to friction, worry and a nervousness around yourself, relationships or a troubling situation, which can be manifesting in anxiety, obsessive thinking, destructive thoughts and behaviours, restless days and sleepless nights.

Heighten your shine: a dull shade of red is inviting you to enter into a state of forgiveness for yourself and others to rekindle the vitality and joy in life you naturally harbour.

ORANGE FOR VITALITY

When bright and beaming, orange is energetically as delicious and juicy as its namesake fruit, speaking of an energy of good health, vigour, vitality, a love of life, a thrill-seeker and a being who is filled with pure, unadulterated joy.

If orange dances its way into your field of light, it is singing to you to get excited, for it brings within its rays messages of happy, exciting times. A healthy hue of orange is also a reflection of your excitable, bouncy social bunny persona – keen to share and produce more of that high vibe with others. You are a natural leader and one who is easily followed and incredibly more-ish! Yummy!

Orange also shines through to highlight your thoughtful and considerate nature, and lights the way to a state of ambition and success that's coming into your path; so choose your teammates with care, for those aligned with your vibe will make for a fun trip, while those coming along for the ride will do so while making no effort other than for what they can energetically draw from you.

WHEN IN SHADE

When orange is present but the colour lacks freshness, moving into shades of muddy brown, it feels exactly like that – indicating a deficit of creativity, productivity and courage in your otherwise usually radiant character. As a knock-on effect, you can feel lacking in growth, freshness or stagnant energetically.

The seemingly heavy or dull vibrations of an orange/orange-brown ray of light can be calling for you to release poor habits or addictions, be these in your ways of thinking or relating to money or addictive pleasures or compulsions, whether these relate to social media, technology, overthinking an argument or even the need to spend money to fulfil yourself.

Heighten your shine: when this heavenly shade is off-centre, we can feel incredibly lazy, sluggish and irritable, and start to starve ourselves of all that brings us joy and pleasure. To refresh yourself, plant new ideas and encourage fresh thinking – and get outside!

YELLOW FOR RADIANCE
(SUB-COLOUR GOLD)

Dear mellow yellow, the colour of the sun, that radiant beam of hope in all our lives. Just as we welcome the sunlight into our eyes, so we subconsciously gravitate towards and welcome those with yellow rays of energy into our lives.

Yellow rays and vibes are held by the creative, the curious, the friendly, the playful, the relaxed. Think of a playful little puppy – easy comes, easy goes, taking life one stride at a time. If you are bathed in yellow rays you are the embodiment of laughter (and we all know how fizzy that feels!), radiating inspiration and optimism. Your energy is contagious and there is an air of freedom in your aura and being.

But it's not all just light and games and 'silliness' for those in this flow. For just as the sun shines light, it does so with purpose – for without sunlight, there is no life. Yellow vibe beings can shine that light and ignite warmth, joy and play in all they meet, bringing much needed warmth and social fire. If this is your vibe and others at first push you away, remember they may have been keeping themselves apart from the joy of life for such a long time that your fizzy vibe feels quite possibly blinding. Never dull down your ray to help them stay emotionally boxed in – burn, baby, burn, and burn bright!

Just as the sun shines with purpose, there a wisdom, a peace that flows deep within those on this frequency – a spiritual advancement and wisdom. So let it flow and don't overthink it – trust your inner flow.

SUB-COLOUR GOLD

When yellow high vibes up into gold, this is a sign of angelic and spiritual protection, a richness in all things you touch. Embrace these heavenly gifts as they fall to you and in whatever guise they may appear!

WHEN IN SHADE

If your vibes are yellow but on the shady side, just like when the sun passes behind a cloud, you could be said to be feeling overcast, be that by life or perhaps you are living too much in your head and under the shade of your thinking. This is particularly telling when fearfulness, carelessness or irresponsibility have crept into your behaviour or choices, be that decision-making at work or even in your diet. That 'anything goes' mentality can fall into self-destructive patterns if not kept in check.

Heighten your shine: if this hue is shady, it's time to rebalance and find a state of stability. Check in and ask yourself what is causing you to feel clouded.

GREEN FOR NURTURING

Green is to go, go, go! The vibe of the doer, the nurturer, the giver, the grower! Ah, it's the fresh-air energy associated with our lungs and hearts.

This is a sign of the well balanced, the heart-led, the patient and the flexible. You are a natural healer – just sitting somewhere near you or passing by your aura is soothing to all other souls right now. You are the flexible beam, in a comfortable, happy, healthy and peaceful state and stage of your life. Even better, you are in a period of growth, fertility and change, so use this wisely and with the patience with which you have been blessed under this colour.

Your animal, intuitive instincts are set to 'on', which is super-cool as you can sniff out opportunity and truth. Your natural vibe is that of the social inquirer, but be mindful of who you are drawn towards. As a doer and a grower, keen green beams can also lean in towards 'fixing' others, as they are so generous with themselves and their time and feel a social responsibility in doing so. Just remember, you must always fix yourself first.

WHEN IN SHADE

You may find yourself flowing in insecurity, jealousy, guilt and envy, and this is weighing on your growth. As a result, you may have taken to act selfishly, digging up the fresh soil that your green roots have been lovingly growing deep within, and looking for past resentments in an attempt to make your ills rather than your joys fresh again!

A cloud in your green can also reflect that you are being too materialistic, so check on in with how that online shopping habit is going – how many 'things' are you accumulating just because can you can, rather than because you need to?

Heighten your shine: one good way to bring this shade into balance is to look at the fortune of others and quite simply celebrate it and spread growth!

BLUE FOR EXPRESSION

To be in the blue is the height of compete coolness – you are officially a cool dude. You are vibing in a peaceful, cool, calm attitude in a free-thinking fashion. You have an ability to express and communicate clearly, and to be on point – this is the colour associated with the throat after all – with the honesty and serenity you tend to energetically and emotionally hold.

This is the colour of those with artistic qualities or those embracing an artistic project. Being artistic doesn't just mean you are a dab hand with the paint brush; you can be creative with language, with words, with organisational skills, with people, so it's important that you seek and sink deeper into what creativity means to you beyond the dictionary definition.

It's also the colour that connects with your intuition – a knowing that what moves through you is more than you and an ability to explore this intuitive part of yourself without the need for a manual. You are a spiritual seeker with an imagination alive with potential.

WHEN IN SHADE

When you are out of the brightness and the colour of this energy is muted and cloudy, you can be said to 'have the blues', which can turn the enlightened you into the moody you. There might be a tendency to be controlling rather than your usual free-flowing, selfless self and to start to be critical and mistrustful of other things and beings.

Heighten your shine: to bring this shade back into balance, write it down, sing it out, record yourself getting off your chest whatever you need to. Clear the communication pipes by blasting them with noise – don't fear what's causing the clog!

TURQUOISE TO SHINE AND HEAL

This is such a special colour to hold within your vibe. When you are swimming in the Caribbean Sea of turquoise blue in your energies, you are in a deep state of spiritual connection and as a result you may reach out towards the healing arts as a career or hobby, either consciously or subconsciously. This is a wonderfully powerful and rare vibe to be flowing in – a reminder of just how unique you are, and a sign that you have achieved a magical sense of balance within your psyche. This is a destination that most are striving towards, so wear it with pride.

It's time to remember what makes you special, but that doesn't mean being self-centred or arrogant – we are all special in our own right and in our own ways. Remember always that there is a wide spectrum of who and what a healer is, so consider also how you bring that magic to others without depleting yourself – and do more of it to heighten your shine!

This is also a colour that denotes that the tides of prosperity are turning back towards you or are already with you now, so dive in – it's time to reclaim your treasure.

WHEN IN SHADE

This colour is so rarely in shade, for it is the pinnacle of achievement. However, if you do feel or sense a cloud moving over your clearer waters, it suggests that you are swimming out into other people's waters and in an envious fashion.

Heighten your shine: get back to counting your blessings to restore your sophisticated shine!

INDIGO, PURPLE AND VIOLET FOR AWARENESS AND SENSITIVITY

These are the colours of the curious, the gentle and the spiritually connected. This is a vibe and an energy that inspires others to do and be good. If these are colours you are alive with, focus on your gifts as a speaker, a teacher, an artist in your field or whichever crop you are growing or nurturing. Often these purple rays are a nod of colour to those who are very psychic without even really knowing it.

Those flowing in the rich and warming tones of purple vibes are sensitive, wise, aware and deeply kind – and they sprinkle that stuff around like magic. They spend much of their time swimming within their depths and should seek to be around those who mirror their kindness and selflessness, so as to protect and honour their own child-like innocence. Be gentle with this light flow – it is precious.

If you are in a violet light, you are extra sensitive, but in all the right ways – an embodiment of all the above. This energy light is also intellectually wise and superbly independent.

WHEN IN SHADE

If your purple light is patchy, cloudy or murky in colour, ask yourself how honest you are being. For this can indicate the telling of the lies (no matter how tiny) and the false truths that we are holding in our flow. They don't have to be nasty lies, just the ways in which you are lying to yourself about how much you really want to be in this job or in that friendship group. It's also a strong indicator that self-insulation has turned into self-absorption.

Heighten your shine: get out of your head and get back to your truth – and honestly so.

GREY AND BLACK FOR PROTECTION

It's agreed by society, isn't it, that black and grey hues are dull and lifeless? Well, the truth is that if these colours shine, this signals an energy of protection, intelligence and reliability. That may not be everyone's bag, but does reliable and safe really always have to be thought of as boring? No! And perhaps black and grey are shining through to you today because very cleverly your energy has gone into safe mode – self-protection mode – so you could ask why this is so. And from what or whom? From yourself, perhaps, or situations that have got heavy?

In closing good news, these colours are also a sign of those who exhibit a classy nature!

WHEN IN SHADE

Just like a storm cloud, grey–black murky energy light denotes anger, tension, confusion and someone who is leaning deeply into the doom and gloom. Ask yourself where you are being unforgiving. Where does it hurt? Allow the sunshine to burn off that which makes you sad.

When grey and black glow in such a way, this can also suggest a past-life hurt and the need to let go of

something you do not even realise you are harbouring –
an energy stowaway! Acknowledge that you are ready
and willing to surrender or release the need to hold on to
this vibe.

Heighten your shine: let yourself be helped – a little less
'me' and a little more 'we' will go a long way; you've done it
alone for long enough.

WHITE AND SILVER FOR CHILDHOOD WONDER

This is a colour that denotes the energy of those as graceful as a swan. It's a colour that brings blessings of goodness, and acts as a totem for those people with an energetical and emotional purity, akin to the innocence of childhood.

People with this colour have a freshness to them: being in their presence is to feel as though you have just opened a window in the stuffiest room of the house. But they don't stop there – they diffuse that vibe through each and every room in every house they walk through.

White and silver light also signals those of high spiritual achievement, those who are well able to get out of 'their head' in the holistic sense, through meditation, good thought, action or deed.

When the white and silver light is not consistent but flashes in amongst other colours within your aura and your vibe, like little angels changing through another colour, this indicates 'newness' – a new opportunity, new life and new arrivals, be that good news or even babies ... Embrace it!

WHEN IN SHADE

When your white or silver rays are glowing in a drab manner, this can be an indication that you have had a heavy night – too much booze, too much sugar and too much indulgence in things we would term socially naughty.

Heighten your shine: hydrate, sleep and take the time to restore.

You are a beautiful mass of rainbow-coloured, high-vibing, far-flowing energy.

Learning to 'See' Your Aura

Learning the language of your rainbow allows you to tap into the energy coding of your life.

So now comes the joyous time where we start to put our Now Age knowledge into practice. It's time to investigate your own aura – to see it, to feel it and to start to understand and connect with it! These next three exercises have been created to help you layer your learning. And just like the layers of your aura, we will be learning in stages.

This might be your first time tuning into your aura and you may be able to see it clearly straightaway, but don't be disappointed if you don't 'see' in the way that you might have expected or imagined you would. This doesn't mean that you 'can't'; it just means we need to dive deeper into exploring 'how'. What we really need to cultivate is trust and self-belief – that what you are 'seeing' and feeling is right *to you*.

As unique beings, we will all have different ways of 'seeing' our auras. Some of us will be able to do it with our eyes open from the get-go, while others may find it more effective to have their physical eyes closed and to sink into their third eye or their spiritual, intuitive sight. One day, it may work one way and the next another, because we and our energy are ever-changing.

'Seeing' in this sense isn't like looking down at your phone or out at the view before you. It can be, absolutely, but for most people, it's a process of going inwards and connecting with your intuition and your mind's eye, and then 'seeing' from within out onto the world. It's like wearing your own Magic Eye glasses: you start to see things that were there the whole time, but you just need to change the lenses and your focus first. (Do you remember those Magic Eye books where you have to let your eyes almost lose focus to allow the hidden image to come into focus? Literally ... magic!)

It is important to know that whether we are seeing with our human eyes open or closed, we are all really looking with our mind's eye – our third eye. Our third eye is our place of spiritual sight which is located on our forehead, between our brows. It's more than an energy centre; it's a place of deep knowing and seeing. It's a place that you have often visited perhaps without realising it – maybe in a daydream or deep sleep, because it's the sweet spot where we communicate with our most loyal ally, our intuition.

Our intuition, often known as our sixth sense, is like a second breath that moves through our body, guiding us lovingly. Intuition exists at the other end of the spectrum to ego: intuition says we can do it, highlights where we have become stuck and leads us to work our way through to the other side. Most of us are not taught how to embrace our intuition, but all we need to do is dial the volume of the ego back and let intuition shine through.

The reason we will be accessing our intuition in the exercise in this chapter is because it connects us to the bigger picture of the universe and spirit. When we move into the mind's eye in these practices, we are not only opening an exciting door that allows us to connect with a marvellous part of ourselves, we are opening our own way of 'seeing' the 'bigger picture' – and then learning to trust that it is right.

The only way you will know how to do this is to have a go, and to practice and play with it – which is what these next exercises are all designed for: to tap into your unique way of 'seeing' and to strengthen these new ways. There are three stages to these practices and I will be guiding you through them; however, you should also know that these practices are part of a toolkit and not a box-ticking exercise!

The other thing to know is that you may 'feel' or sense your energy and its colour at first, so that's why we'll start by gently feeling for your aura. This is the first step towards seeing your aura, for if you know what it feels like, your intention and intuition will then know what you are 'looking' for.

I recommend starting with the first exercise and practising it daily for a minimum of three days before you move on to the next. Once you have moved through all the exercises, you can go through each practice daily, finding your own flow. You will know if you are doing too much (if and when frustration kicks in) and you will likewise know if you are doing too little (for instance, if you feel as if you can't be bothered to try – remember, that's the ego trying to keep you safe and in the confines of the so-called 'norm').

Safety Instructions:

Not suitable for children.

Take care when placing your aroma dish in the centre of the lamp.

Do not drop the oil outside the dish area.

Do not touch the bulb when plug in, be aware of the heated bulb.

IMPORTANT:

This AQUALINA Mini Touch Lamp is using 220v voltage, please note it cannot be used in 110v countries.

If the light bulb runs out, TURN OFF YOUR LAMP, UNPLUG and ALLOW TO COOL FOR 15 minutes.

Then simply take off the warmer dish and metal housing and you can replace the bulb. Replacement bulbs are available at sales@grangestreet.com

Warranty:

This AQUALINA's Aroma Touch Lamp comes with a 1 year carry in warranty. If you are having any problems with your device, please contact our Customer Service Centre at +44 1892 710290 or email sales@grangestreet.com for assistance.

Note:

This warranty only covers defects arising from the normal and proper operation of the product and will not cover faults coming into existence as a result of external damage to the product or misuse.

AQUALINA's reserves the right to alter the warranty without prior notice.

AQUALINA®

Mini Aroma Touch Lamp
User Manual

Brighten up your life and aromatise your home environment with AQUALINA's one of a kind Mini Aroma Touch Lamp.

Simply add a few drops of the free scented oil accessory and with a simple touch you can sit back and enjoy the beautiful light and matching aroma.

Features:

- Touch Lamp and Aroma Oil Burner / Melting Wax Lamp
- Material: Metal
- 3 Levels of Lamp Brightness
- Power: ~25W
- Voltage: AC 220V only
- Product Size: 11 x 15cm

Operating Instructions:

1. Place a few drops of the scented oil or place one or more sections of a scented bar into the warmer dish
2. Plug in the lamp to a 220V socket
3. Simply touch the lamp anywhere to turn on
4. Touch the lamp again to increase the brightness. There are 3 brightness settings
5. To turn off the lamp simply touch again

Layer 1: Feeling Your Energy – Your Aura as an Energy Ball

Feeling is believing with energy, so you can repeat this stage as often as you like because it's fun, but also as a reminder that your energy and your aura is 'there'. The more aware we become of our aura – and you've guessed it – the more we trust, feel and 'see' it.

I like to do this exercise most mornings to check where my energy is at and to also remind myself that I am more than just what I may see before me in the mirror. This exercise brings a greater awareness of energy and I feel there is no better way to start my day than with this energy kick – a yummy, energy alternative to coffee!

These practices are all personal to you, though, so you can do this exercise at any time of the day. If you find that it's better for you to do it just before you hit the sleep button because you have unwound from the day and you are more relaxed, then do that. Most important is that you do it somewhere quiet or peaceful and also comfortable (which is why my bed is often my preferred space!). As you start to practise your aura work in one dedicated space, you are also inviting in a very sacred energy to that space and, over time, just walking towards or thinking of that space will provide you with great comfort.

- If this is your first time doing this exercise, please sit comfortably, either on a chair with your feet planted on the floor, or seated cross-legged on a cushion or the floor. This is to ground your energy to the Earth, so you feel strong and supported in your practice. Once you have performed this exercise five or six times and you are more than comfortable with it, you can take it out into everyday life with you, but for now ... root in!

· Rub your hands together approximately five times back and forth at speed, with some pressure between them (much like when you have just come in from the cold and are trying to bring some heat back to your body).

· After the last rub, hold your hands close together and take a long breath in and out.

· Very slowly, really slowly, start to pull your hands apart – you can close your eyes if that helps. Keep moving your hands apart until it feels or looks as if you have the length of a shoebox between your hands. Hold there for a few breaths.

· Then, at the same speed that you moved your hands out, start to move them back towards each other until you feel the weight or the thickness of the energy between your hands.

· That right there is *your* energy – your aura, your vibe, your energy! You have created an energy ball!

· Fret not if you don't feel it on your first attempt – it can take a few rounds to 'get it' and to allow the mind and the sceptical ego to settle down. If you tried this with your eyes open, try with them closed next time, or if you had them closed, try it with them open! In all cases, take your time go slow!

You can also use this energy ball for your further benefit. For example, once I feel the energy ball, I then move my hands further away from each other, expanding the energy ball at the same time. Next, I lightly place my hands and therefore my energy over my eyes (or over any part of my body that needs a little extra TLC) and move my fresh energy into that space just by laying it there. Placing it over your eyes is a great starting point as it's like splashing cold water in your face – refreshing and energetically invigorating – but explore where else may feel good for you to place your energy today!

Layer 2: Seeing Your Energy

From feeling it, we now naturally progress to seeing your energy and your aura. The next layer of learning comes in seeing the subtleties of our energy with our physical eyes. This practice allows you to perceive the light of your energy, before we introduce its colour. It will strengthen your understanding of what your energy looks like and will help later when we delve into the mind's eye to explore the colours and texture of our aura and her vibes.

We'll start again with small steps, using our hand as our 'model' and then expand our vision to explore the whole of our energy body.

You will need a few simple props: a white wall or sheet of white paper, or a mirror, to help you see your energy against its surface.

- Come to sit in your peaceful space – either on a chair, feet planted onto the ground, or cross-legged on a cushion or on the floor – in front of a white wall or with your piece of white paper or mirror before you, ideally at eye level so you are not straining your neck.
- Taking a soothing breath, allowing yourself to arrive into your space: start by sparking your energy ball, as you did in the exercise on pages 75–7 – rubbing your hands together and moving them outwards and then inwards until you feel your energy once more. It's important that we get the energy dancing so it's a little easier to start to see it.
- Then hold your dominant hand (the hand you write with) in front of, but not flat against, the white wall, sheet of paper or mirror.

- Focus on your fourth finger (the ring finger). If you are using the mirror, look at your physical hand and not the reflection of your hand. However, if another finger is intuitively calling for your attention, lead with that – there is no wrong way only your right way.
- Look at the tip of your fourth finger and then slowly start to move your gaze off towards the left of the centre of your fingertip. This is a tiny, tiny movement, so go slow and *breathe*.
- As you do this, your other fingers move lightly into your peripheral vision and you start to become aware of them – they may be a little blurry.
- As you breathe, relax and hold that viewpoint. With your physical eyes, you will start to see a little light, perhaps a shadow, which is white or greying in colour or texture, radiating around, off or from your fingers, as though your fingers have a shadow all around them. It's a shadow of light: this is your etheric body, the layer of the aura closest to the body.
- Your mind will tell you that it's just your vision out of focus. That's ok – that's what the ego is there for: to keep you within your 'norm'.
- To start with, your eyes may hurt or you may be able to hold this for a long period of time, so come in and out of it. *Play* with it – make this practice fun, and allow yourself to smile when you start to see it. No matter how quickly or fleeting it may seem, the more you affirm, the more you allow yourself to experience this new way of 'seeing'. The more you allow yourself to acknowledge that you are more than you know, the more you will surrender to the experience and 'see'.

- When you feel that you are starting to get more confidence in seeing the light body around your hands, you can take it up a notch and go 3D.
- Very slowly start to move your head around your hand as if you have 3D goggles on and you are seeing your hand for the very first time – and in a sense, you are really 'seeing' your hand and its aura in all its glory for the very first time.
- Move your head in and out around your fingertips so that your gaze keeps moving in and out – you are now looking deeper into the aura around your fingertips. If you lose it, don't worry; just go back a step and progress at your own pace. In time, when you 'lose it', you'll be able to reset your eyes just by blinking and picking back up where you left off.
- When you 'have it', start to move your head back and away from your hand to expand your viewpoint, moving out towards the other layers of aura. You may already start to see colours, but that does takes time, practice and patience. If you don't, remember that what's most important is that you are starting to witness your aura, your vibe and your energy.
- Please also pay attention to the sensation in your hands. The more aware you become of your aura and your energy, the more you will start to sense it, so be open to feeling for any pins and needles, pulses or prickles, hot and cool sensations that are starting to make their way through your fingertips and hands. Note everything down as this reinforces what you see and is great to reflect on during those days when it feels a little harder to get to 'seeing'.

When you are seeking to see your aura, it's important to start with your hands or smaller areas of your body, so that you can gain confidence in what you are seeing and feeling (this too will come with practice) and your mind doesn't just write it off as 'nonsense'. Remember that ego has kept you small for years to keep you safe, so don't blame it – just work towards expanding into your intuition as you move through these practices. Your intuition is guiding you even when you are not aware of it.

You can also practice this exercise on plants, your animals and your loved ones, because all living things have an aura or body of light (yes, that's right we all have a halo!), just as you do. In the summer, you could head to the park, lie on the grass with the sky as your white wall and practise on the plants and the trees – it's utterly therapeutic!

Layer 3: Expanding Your View

It's time to widen the view to see the bigger picture and to envisage your aura around your entire body, not just your hand. This is really no different to the work you've done so far – it's just an expansion of it, so take the pressure off yourself. Witnessing your aura around your whole body is simply about strengthening your gaze and trusting in yourself and your intuition. Every exercise is gently working intuitive muscles that you've perhaps never felt before so repetition is key. Stick to the three-day rule of thumb when diving into your exercises.

This exercise is a little like looking at a Magic Eye pattern again. We are so used to seeing a reflection of how we look day to day through the filter of our mind. For instance, I have blonde hair, blue eyes, freckles and a body that could do with losing a little weight here and toning up there – that's the imprint of my reflection on my mind and it's not always completely honest or true. However, our mind is not always a kind filter and we tend to fixate on a mental image of ourselves and pay more attention to that image than we do our actual reflection. Realistically, how much time do you spend really looking at yourself in the mirror, gazing deep into your eyes, acknowledging all your great features, and sending love to the parts you have loathed for one reason or another?

The eyes are the key to the soul, they say, through which we get to glimpse someone's true nature, but we can see this too in our energy field, our aura. Let's take some time out and look a little deeper to see beyond that 'standardised' version of self we hold. You may wish to read these instructions over a few times before you try this exercise. Or my favourite way is to record yourself reading it on your phone so you can guide yourself all the more clearly.

· Find a comfortable sitting position once again. You can play calming music but ideally without words (words can be distracting as the mind can wander off to words, away from the task at hand). This time, though, you will need to sit in front of a mirror – a full-length mirror, if possible, for it is time to see yourself in all your glory! If the mirror is against a white wall, that's even better, though it's no problem if not.
· I like to sit cross-legged in front of the mirror, or on a chair with my feet planted on to the ground, but you should find your own comfort zone as you might be here for long periods of time. If you would rather stand, that's fine too!
· Rub your hands together once again to awaken your energy and spark your energy ball. Close your eyes, take a breath and place your hands on your lap, palms face open: this is a spiritual signal that you are open to receiving from your aura, from the universe, from spirit or whatever you have come to know this power to be. Allow yourself to settle into the moment, to arrive in the here and now.
· After a moment, open your eyes and look yourself directly in the eye, in your reflection in the mirror. (It's not going to be for long so let the awks wash away from you with your breath.)
· Now, just as you did with your fourth, (ring) finger, start to move your gaze towards the left of your

face *super-slowly* until the reflection of your nose comes into view and your eyes are in your peripheral vision. Hold this space, take long steady breaths in and out as you allow your etheric body to come into view off to the left of your head.

· Once you can 'see' the energy, be that a haze of light or a flickering (remember that it is super-subtle and not an advertising board!), it's time to expand your range.

· On an inhale, start to lean back away from the mirror for a count of one. Hold here and allow yourself to witness the energy of your aura. Move further back for another count of one. Hold, breathe, look, feel – let all the senses take you into your aura. If you lose it or feel you have lost it, take a break and start this step again. Take your time – remember this is not going to all come on day one for most people, so give yourself time to practise. With patience, you will find how to surrender and find your own way of seeing the subtle vibe of your aura.

· If your mind chatters to you that you 'can't', my favourite life mantra is: '*I am, and I can*.' Repeat it out loud or in your mind three times. (Three is a powerful spiritual number – you will notice we are doing a lot in threes because this number represents creation, manifestation and growth, and also symbolises the powerful and intricate connection between mind, body and spirit.) This will help you to tap into your intuition or your psyche – and it's a practice that has seen me through many a tough mental spot!

- Go explore and expand now. You know what you are doing – move or lean back as far as feels comfortable to you and let your breath support you as you open your mind. Change the angle as you did with your hand. *Play* with it and have fun!

You may be starting to witness colours already or you may not. It doesn't matter. How we 'see' in this way is mainly generated though our third eye. It's a unique form of perception that you can learn to add gently to your everyday life. Some people will also *hear* the colours because intuition and spirit sing through us in many ways, so be open to however this experience comes to you and don't fixate on how you think it should.

You might find it important to note down your experiences after each practice as a log of how far you have come and a reminder of how brilliantly you are doing – as well as helping you put more power into what's to come next ... We've added some pages at the back for you to jot it down!

Expanding Your Practice: Going Within to Look Without

We've talked a lot about the third eye and intuition, and now it's time to really grab that connection and run freely with it – it's time to witness your colour-coding!

In the next exercise, we will move deeper within, into the third eye so that you can 'see' through your inner sight and your intuitive knowing. For now, I would ask you to stay with this practice for three days as you are strengthening your trust in yourself and the universe, as well as deconditioning yourself of years of misleading beliefs. Soon you will be able to move between the exercises freely, at your leisure and at any time.

I recommend that you read through this exercise each step at a time and let your mind's eye open while your physical eyes remain open; let the words act as a guide to take you where you need to 'see' from within. You can also record yourself reading the steps and play this back to listen in and help yourself sink deeper under – but please don't do this until you have read and worked through the steps at least three times! You can also have a friend or loved one guide you by reading the words; a little like storytelling, powerful stuff happens with energy and our aura when we share and connect like this – and remember that your aura loves an energy hug from another being when they are on your vibe. However, in time you won't need to follow the words.

· You can sit on the floor or in a chair or lie down on the floor or on a bed for this one – wherever comfort greets you. Come to the breath: take a long breath in through the nose, then a long breath out through the nose. With each breath, your body is surrendering to what is beneath it, be that the chair, the bed or the ground.

· Allow your eyes to become heavy. Your attention and breath moves inwards, towards the heart. Take five breaths, each for a count of seven, in and out through the nose.

· When you are ready, float your breath and your attention up towards your mind's eye, your third eye – the centre of your brow or forehead. With every breath, start to surrender to the feelings and the sensations that start to trickle in through here.

· Softly repeat three times, either in your mind or out loud: 'I am my intention, I surrender to see all the vibrant, vibrating colours of me.'

· Allow yourself to visualise, sense or feel a ball of silver–white light, no bigger than a tennis ball, bouncing down onto your mind's eye – your forehead. (Sometimes this ball will bounce on your heart or another of your energy centres; if it does, allow it to do so. Please remember there is no wrong, only your right.) With every breath, the height from which the ball bounces increases until the ball of energy – the ball of light – cracks open like an egg.

· Your breath allows that fresh energy to travel up and down your body, soothing as it goes. Now, your breath allows the energy to expand and open up to form an auric dome all over and around your body. (This might look like a tent or another encapsulating and comforting structure; as we've seen, there is no wrong so let what comes, come!) This is your viewing gallery and your energy is dancing safely and confidently, powerful around and within this dome or this tent, the edges of which shine around you like a halo as a peaceful darkness fills the space.

- Two things may happen next. You may stay in the dome where you find yourself in the room – lying or sitting as you were – or your third eye may lift you to the roof or side of the dome so that you are looking back at yourself and your physical body.
- Watch now … surrender now … allow the colours of self to start moving in and around the dome, in no particular order, at varying speeds. Let them come; take your time. You may see many colours, you may see one or two … that's all good.
- Come to ask of your aura, set your intention by softly repeating three times: '*I allow myself to see the colours, or the colour, of my layer 1.*'
- Breathe, allow and witness. Don't just 'look' in your mind's eye, but surrender to hearing the colour or feeling for it. Perhaps it comes to you as a flash of colour or is shown to you as a piece of fruit with the same colour or a name, or even a piece of clothing or household item that relates to the colour of this layer. (Remember that you, your intuition and your energy are made of intelligent stuff!)
- When you feel it – see it, acknowledge it. Say the colour in your mind or out loud.
- Now to layer 2 of your aura we flow. The intention remains; simply tweak it to: '*I allow myself to see the colours, or the colour, of my layer 2.*' As before, repeat for a total of three times. Repeat the process

- breathe, set your intention to allow yourself to see, witness what comes and acknowledge it.
· Repeat these steps for each of your seven layers. Ask to see each one, witness it as it is shown to you, however that may be – and note it mentally.
· When you reach layer 7 of your aura, repeat these steps again. Then repeat your intention three times: 'I allow myself to the colours, or the colour, of my layer 7'. Breathe, allow, witness and then acknowledge internally or out loud as before, but hang out in this layer as long as you want now. Remember this is the sweet spot, this is the seventh heaven after all! Pay attention to your visions, your feelings, for they are magical messengers here.
· When you are ready to come back to the here and now – the present – take a long breath in through the nose and this time breathe out through your open mouth (stick your tongue out too) and sigh it all out.
· Now begin to count backwards from seven. Take a breath in for a count of seven and out for a count of seven for each number, moving back through each layer. Each number, each count and each breath moves you back down or through each layer of your aura: layer 7 (inhale, exhale), 6 (inhale, exhale), 5 (inhale, exhale), 4 (inhale, exhale), 3 (inhale, exhale), 2 (inhale, exhale) and 1 (inhale, exhale).
· As we reach layer 1, become aware of your fingers, your toes, your body, your position within the room and your surroundings. Take a long breath, cleansing in and out along the spine – and you are home. Affirm three times: 'I am totally energised, totally safe, totally protected.'

If you feel heavy or light-headed, please ground yourself – eat something or take a walk – and then remember to write down the story of the colours and the layers you felt or saw.

Over time, as your confidence grows and you can relax without the need to enter such a meditative state, you can start to practise flowing through each layer with your eyes wide open, again using the mirror but without the written steps as your guide.

Seeing Another Person's Aura

You can now expand your skills a little further to explore the energy of others. Yes, that's right, we can also use these exercises to read another person's energy. You can do it with any of the exercises but the best one to start with is 'Layer 3: Expanding Your View'. Instead of the mirror and your own reflection, you can ask your loved one or friend to sit opposite you. Again, for ease, sit them in front of a white wall.

In time, you will be able to do this exercise out and about in the real world, even when sat at a bar, but be mindful of the amount of energy that you are open and exposed to, and keep within your practice zone until you really feel you are comfortable and confident about working with your own aura and energy. We can become like sponges and need to ensure we are in control of what energetically is coming our way.

For the 'Going Within to Look Without' exercise, just change the intention at the fourth step. Open the energy dome but allow the other person to be your subject rather than yourself. Visualise them sitting or lying by you and repeat three times: *'[Their name] is my intention, I surrender to see all the colours of their love, their truth, their vibe, their layers.'* You can work with a photo of the person too – this will help to deepen the connection. Always remember, though, that when we read others, it should not be for our own personal gain, only for better understanding. It's not for control, only for love and a deepened connection. Explain to them why you are doing this, what it will do for them and verbalise what you receive as this comes to you.

When you are looking at another aura, you will need to be extra aware of the signals your intuition is sending to you to flag to you what feels 'good' and what feels 'off'. You may feel warming, comforting prickles through your body, or perhaps your intuition will light a smile in your face when another energy feels good; but if your face tightens and frowns, this is a sign that the energies of this person at this moment are not intermingling well with yours. Now, this does not necessarily mean that person is a bad person – this is your energy just flagging to you to step back. You can investigate deeper and add to your intentions: 'Why is this energy not good for mine?' Repeat this three times to allow your energy to show you why, either through your mind's eye or through your body and its sensors, or both. You can also ask, repeating three times, 'Should I step back or completely away from their energy?' and allow your energy to tell you about this too.

You can also use these exercises to heal or soothe your aura and your interactions with another, which we will be looking at in more detail in the next chapter.

It's time to see the magnitude of beauty you truly are.

Taking Care of
Your Aura

Even if your energies are feeling bright right now, you are always allowed to add more light to your sparkle!

Just like washing our hair, moisturising our skin and eating the right diet to take care of our physical bodily layers, we can and should tend to the care of our aura – our energy body. Even if your energies are light right now, you can still add more light to your sparkle!

That's not all. In keeping our energies clear and on high, we don't just feel good and look better internally and externally, we also change the frequency of our magnetisation and therefore what we attract towards us. We draw in what we really need and who we really need, as well as fulfilling our desires – if they are for our highest good, of course! We can magnetically attract the right job or the right partner by feel and by frequency – and not simply by how they look or what our ego thinks they can offer. We can also release and surrender anyone or anything that is no longer serving our vibe and our auric flow.

So let's explore a full, layer-by-layer colour cleanse, as well as look at some quick tips for lifting your vibe on the go. It's true we live in a world where we are constantly 'on', but we have the power to take time and to make a change, whether we commit to thirty minutes of meditation or thirty seconds of auric smiling or an auric brush with some sweet-smelling sage.

As for the last chapter, you can read through the next exercise as a step-by-step guide and tap into your mind's eye with your physical eyes wide open, or you can record yourself reading each step – or even better, have a friend or loved one recite the steps for you.

Cleanse and Protect Your Aura: Set It to Attract What You Desire and Need

You've now 'seen' your layers in all their glory, it's time to cleanse these layers and vibe them up using your newly honed skills to go a little deeper into your aura. I would recommend doing this exercise at least once a week to keep on top of your energies while you explore these practices. Then, when you are familiar with them, maintain your energies by doing this exercise once a month. However, if life has thrown you and you feel off-kilter, please do it when you need to.

Just as when you went inwards to see and review your auric layers in the last chapter, you can go inwards and review them with the intention of lightening up the colour and brightness of each vibe. You can let go of what's been clogging your flow and set your vibes to the right frequency for manifesting and attracting your desires – be that attracting the right job, right partner, right pals or to assist you in making the right choices in love, life and work. You can focus on a vibe within a particular layer of interest to boost your health, heal and heighten your emotions, connect with kindred spirits, or to manifest with the universe right beside you.

Even if you may not know what you 'want' right now (and that's ok), by setting your frequency towards one of love, you will draw in all things heartfelt, loving and kind, and there is real magic to be had in watching what life brings to you when you are surfing the right wavelengths.

Where you can, have a bath or shower before this exercise – washing your crown, your head, your hair. Water is amazing for washing away the soot formed by negative thoughts (yours or another's) and external energies (of your boss, the energy of the people on the bus next to you), and anything not serving you or low in vibe.

Use this written exercise as a guide for at least three runs, and then you can record it or have someone guide you through it if you wish.

- Get comfy! If you are seated, rest your back against a wall or sit in a chair with a back. If you are lying down, take to the floor or bed, but prop pillows under your neck, knees and feet – relaxation is key here!
- Lay one hand on your heart and the other on your belly. Focus on lengthening your breath in and out through your nose. Take that breath in through the heart and then move the breath down into the belly – your aim is to lift your hand on your heart and your hand on your belly with this luscious, fulfilling breath cycle. This will aid in deepening the flow.
- Let your eyes gently close (if you are not reading these steps as a guide). Find comfort in the darkness behind your closed eyelids. Once more, with every breath, you are coming deeper and deeper into your heart. Take three long, cleansing breaths in through the nose and out through the

mouth: you are opening an energy window at your heart, inviting fresh, clear energy into your body and your being.

· Bring your attention to your mind's eye now, sensing, visualising or beginning to feel yourself standing or lying down within your own unique auric or energy dome.

· Take your attention and awareness firmly and directly to the top of the dome – the outer layer. This is usually a pure white iridescent light, but allow this to be shown to you however is right for you today, here and now.

· Start to scan this layer with your breath, watching and feeling for any cloudy, dull rays or patches on or within the dome. Now watch as they effortlessly fade and clear with each and every breath you take.

· Visualise and sense now as hexagonal shapes start to come into view. Notice how these shapes are forming within the outer layer of your dome – each hexagon powerfully connected and interlocked with the other, much like an intricate honeycomb in a beehive. Explore this and allow yourself to become fascinated by it, as if it's the only thing there. Your intention is to watch and explore your energy and, as you continue to do so, you are giving it power purely through setting that intention. This power is creating a strong protective form – a layer of energy that will filter the external energies of people and places and keep them lovingly away from seeping into your aura.

- With every breath, feel the strength and the quality of your dome as it becomes stronger with the arrival of this hexagonal protective light-matrix, which now gently surrounds you.
- Know now that this superstructure is protecting you, sealing you in lovingly and keeping anything out that is not for your good. The unique angles formed by the hexagonal grid are enabling energy photosynthesis to take place, allowing for more universal light and more healthy human light to be drawn in to your aura and allowing for the safe, calm and loving removal of all the energies that are no longer serving you and your energy. Know and affirm three times: '*I am and my energies are protectively sealed in.*' You can breathe happily here and your energies can happily, freely start to flow.
- Turn to your voice now and repeat three times in your mind or out loud, whichever feels right to you: '*Show me the layers of my light, my aura, which need a healing, healthy shine.*' Take your time here; as always, patience is key. Allow the light and its layers to be shown to you in whatever way is right for you; you may see, feel or even hear the colour or the layer, or perhaps see a sign that is representative of the colour and layer. Allow this to come to you; if necessary, keep repeating the invitation over and over again until your energy comes into view.
- Gently take your breath into the colour or layer that is being shown to you, and allow each breath to

cleanse through the light and the layer, as you did with the top layer of the dome. Your breath is like an energy vacuum cleaner, so allow your breath to gather up the soot and the cloud of the layer on an inhale, and, on an exhale, allow that soot to be sent up and through the hexagonal shields of your energy dome. Repeat for three long breaths or until you feel a cool breeze pass over your body, watching as that soot evaporate into nothingness as it is dispelled as soon as it moves near the dome of hexagons.

· If you feel as if you can't quite shift all the cloud, go easy on yourself. Come back tomorrow – little and often is a good rule of thumb as some changes take a bit more time.

· When you are ready to progress, repeat three times more: '*Show me the layers of my light, my aura, which need a healing, healthy shine.*' Then repeat the last couple of steps again, and allow your next layer or colour to be shown, once again clearing and lifting any soot, dullness or cloud from the light and layer with every breath.

· Repeat these steps until no more layers and no more colours are shown to you.

· Be aware that you may only see just the one colour and one layer – or you may see three. Either is more than ok, and make peace with what just needs to be.

· You may now wish to use your aura and your energies to manifest something or to let it go; to enquire as to where in your life you can add more light in order to draw in your heart's desires. To do this, you can change the intention along the following lines: *'Show me the layers of my light, my aura, which need uplifting…*

- *'…to bring in the love of my life.'*
- *'…to bring in my new career path.'*

- Or:
  - *'Show me who or what brings the right energy into my life to allow me to vibe higher.'*

- Consider your wish and simply ask your energies to show it. If, perhaps, you are feeling stagnant and unclear as to what or who is lowering your shine, you can tweak your intention to:
  - *'Show me the layers of my light that need freeing from another's draining.'*
  - *'Show me who or what I need to release from my energies in order to vibe higher – and how.'*

- Whatever the enquiry, simply ask, watch and accept what comes, and then breathe in and through the soot, the dust, the person or situation. Cleanse up and through the top of the dome and send any negative light out through the hexagonal matrix. Where you sense or see that you need more light, with the breath, draw in universal light through the dome to top up your own. You will know it is universal light or light that is 'good for you' as you remind yourself that only good can pass through and into the dome – remember that intention has been set.
- When there are no more layers to be shown or no more paths of enquiry, recite in your mind or out

loud: '*Please show me the rainbow of possibility that I am, in all my rays, in all my glory.*'

· This may take time, so allow the colours of your aura to dance in and around your auric dome, and feel into the emotions, the happy sparks of life going off like fireworks within your body as your energies wash together, as you feel the purest essence that is you powerfully vibing as one – as your aura.

· Stay in this space as long as you need ... take your time. When you are ready, bring your attention, your awareness, back towards your breath and your body and affirming three times: '*I am totally safe, totally protected.*'

Make sure you drink plenty of water after this exercise and spend at least three minutes seated with your feet planted on the ground. It may feel as if you haven't done very much, but you have made great if subtle changes – an energy workout if you will – so go steady, eat something and get grounded!

And note it down. Don't let your fascination with yourself end there. Make sure to take stock and watch how those colours, those layers and those messages start to show themselves to you in the everyday, as your energy sings to you that it and life, the universe, are working and drawing to you the collaboration of your energetical efforts.

Once you have practised this exercise a few times or more, you will be able to fly in to that dome effortlessly just with the breath, a thought, by closing your eyes or opening your mind's eye, even while on the move, but for now settle back and enjoy it when and where you can.

You are your greatest vibe – you deserve to shine as bright as you truly are!

Living with
Your Aura

Repeat after me: I am a full-flowing, high-vibing rainbow of radiating potential.

Sometimes we won't have (or feel we don't have) the extra minutes in the day to do a full check-in on our aura, our vibe. For those days where that feels somewhat impossible, here are some quick-fire tips to brighten your vibe wherever you find your feet!

USE LIGHT TO FIND OR HEIGHTEN YOUR ENERGY

When there is little sunlight beaming through the sky, or it's dark outside and you can't seem to find any bounce to get out of bed, I find a daylight or SAD lamp really gets the light into your body. Your aura responds best to natural light, of course, so if you are feeling in the thick of it or if life is weighing heavy on your energy, get outside or get to the window.

HOW TO GROUND YOURSELF TO DISPEL WORRY AND FIND CALM

Grounding is superbly important in all Now Age and spiritual practices, for when we dive into this work we have to remember to bring the benefits and strength back into the physical body. Tell-tale signs that we are not grounded are feeling wobbly, clumsy, forgetful or a little out of sorts – our energy is powerful but it needs to be rooted in the present moment!

Walking in nature grounds your energy, but even planting your feet into the ground works. Stand tall, hands by your side, with your feet hip-distance apart, and really feel your feet against the floor, plant them into the ground. With every breath that you inhale through the nose and then exhale, visualise that breath moving down and out through your feet into the ground, carrying with it any tension, worry or fear, deep into the Earth's core. Hang out here for a few breaths as you feel the energy of your breath now bring the loving, grounding energy from the Earth's core back into your body, up into your heart. Affirm three times: '*I am totally centred, totally aligned, totally safe, totally protected.*'

WATER VISUALISATION TO CLEAN AWAY ANGER

This next quick hit is great on those days when you've become angered over something seemingly trivial – perhaps someone has knowingly or unknowingly triggered a memory or a feeling from the past that you can energetically investigate at a later time, but for now you need to cool off and wash away the low or bad vibes.

Have a shower (not a bath) and get your head under the water. As you stand under the water's flow, visualise the water falling through each and every one of your seven auric layers before it hits your body, washing them clean as you go, washing away any soot, dust, misheld energy or tension, which then flows down into the plughole with your shampoo suds!

AIR VISUALISATION TO COUNTER HURT AND UPSET

This is one you can do on the spot, any time, anywhere! It's one I do when someone throws me an unhelpful or unkind curveball, so that my energy allows me to remain calm and I can respond with intuition rather than react with ego and upset, hurt or anger. With practice, you can learn to do this while someone is talking to – or rather *at* – you. (We all know those conversations, don't we!)

Firstly, make sure that your feet are flat on the floor (legs uncrossed), held and grounded by the Earth, as in the grounding exercise above.

Breathe in and out through the nose. Take that breath and your attention in towards the heart – this brings in an energy of softness and kindness. Repeat this three times to settle your body.

Then move your awareness and breathe in through the heart and up through your throat, up through your third eye, up and out through your crown. Repeat, breathing in through your heart, up through your throat, through your third eye, up and exhaling out through your crown.

Start to visualise this flow of breath moving out through the crown, blasting up and through the layers of our aura, like smoke from a chimney, shifting out and away from us any soot that unfriendly friends have delivered. Allow it to move up and away before it settles into your being: know that it is only part of you if you allow it and if you accept it. Repeat three to five times before bringing your awareness back to the breath and breathe in and out through the nose. Allow everything to move back to natural, back to neutral. *Smile*. You are good to go!

AFFIRMATIONS TO STRENGTHEN YOUR CONFIDENCE AND BELIEVE IN YOURSELF

How we speak to or about ourselves really affects the frequency of our vibe, energy and our aura. Conversations about our physical appearance, for example, are held in our auric layers, specifically the Astral Body and the Mental Body. In order to release the energies here and change the vibe, we must change the tone of the conversation.

'I am' is the most powerful word combination in this universe. Together, these two words are like a magical word wand, for what follows is what you will create and become in your energy, your mind and in your life. So use them wisely and affirm what you desire to be rather than who you 'think' you are.

Play with them and make your own but here are some for starters:

· *I am beautiful, kind and loving, and I am radiating as such.*
· *I am smarter than I know, braver than I think.*

- *I am a full-flowing, high-vibing rainbow of radiating potential.*
- *I am more than enough.*
- *I am uniquely me.*
- *I am shining.*
- *I am reflecting the energy of the job role that feels amazing to me.*
- *I am attracting only those who seek to bring and to be good energy.*
- *I am releasing all that no longer serves.*
- *I am ...*

... what are you today? You decide and you will become!

Whatever the conversation, whenever you are being cruel with your tongue, stop, take a breath and take charge of the mental conversation. '*I am useless*' becomes '*I am useful*'. '*I am unlovable*' becomes '*I am Love in all its glory*' and so on, as you add to your shine and let the true story be told.

AURIC SMILING TO BOOST YOUR DAY AND INSPIRE GOOD SLEEP

Your emotions have a great effect on your aura, so an auric smile can be a game changer – and it's easy, super-effective and free! By developing and tapping into your auric smile, you can start to release happy endorphins into your body that you then pour into your energies, just setting your intention.

I like to do this by smiling and visualising a rainbow on top of my head. I see my smile expand with every breath I take, reaching each layer of the rainbow and touching every colour as effortlessly as it takes for the smile to cross my face. Does this sound easy? It is! Try it before you head to bed for a colourful and dreamy night's sleep!

EXAMINE YOUR ACTIONS AND FIND YOUR WAY

Our actions, just like our emotions, can affect our vibe and they are also great signals as to whether what we are doing is good and healthy for our energy. Do they fill you with tickles or magic? Hooray, lean deeper in! But perhaps the thought of something feels off? If it does, listen to that too and lean away from it!

When it's time to go on that date, listen to your energy and your vibe: do you feel nervous, excited or do you need to lean into your energies more deeply to explore if this is really the person for you?

Is it time to leave or stay with your job – how does your body feel when you visualise yourself moving in either direction? Always come back to your auric dome when you have a chance to look deeper, but know you have grown so much, and that growth doesn't just exist when you are in front of the mirror or sunk deeply in your healing dome, it is experienced in your everyday life

Doing something kind for yourself, your family, friends or strangers is always a great way to nourish your energy.

Start small; for example, run yourself a bath or buy yourself flowers, hold the door open for a stranger, gift a passer-by your smile – just leave a mark because energetically it's so good for the soul!

Remember, just because it's easy doesn't meant it hasn't got power! Back in the days when life was simpler, these small acts were recognised as richer things.

CHANGE YOUR CLOTHES TO GET YOURSELF IN THE RIGHT MOOD

Your clothes too can change your vibe – they're also great indicators for where you are at energetically. You know when you wake up some mornings and you have an idea about what you want to wear, but when you put it on, it just doesn't feel right? That's because your energy is not in that space today, so check in with your aura and your vibe. If you want to draw more of a certain shade into your aura then wear it, eat food of that colour and immerse your vibe in it. It really is that simple.

If you have a super-important meeting, lean in to your colours: what will radiate your empowerment? If you have party to go to, what colour lifts your mood? Look at your aura in the 'Expanding Your View' practice (see pages 82–5) and affirm three times: 'I allow myself to see which colour will allow me to shine as bright as bright can be.' Allow what comes into your view to appear and honour it through wearing the appropriate colour T-shirt, lipstick or underwear. Bring that life to light through your aura and lighten and empower your mood.

Most importantly of all, listen to yourself. If something makes you smile and that energy lifts you up, then it's good for you. If something is off, listen in and ask what and why.

SMUDGE AND CLEANSE AWAY LOW HANGING VIBES AND INVIGORATE YOUR OWN

You can call on Mother Earth's beauties to help clean your aura by using a sage wand. I do this after every energy session or psychic reading, just to separate out the dust from the individual I have just worked on. It's also good to use if you are feeling tired or heavy, and it can spruce up or sweeten your energies too.

Light the end of the smudging tool. Ideally this should consist of white sage as it is gently effective, or palo santo wood. If you spark a large flame, blow it out so that just the end embers of the sage wand are smouldering and the smoke is drifting from the end of the wand into the atmosphere around you.

Then 'dust' your body with the smoke from the sage wand. Just as the breath in the 'Cleanse and Protect Your Aura' meditation (see pages 99–105) gathers up the negative energy and lifts it back to the universe, the smoke from the wand does this for you here. Use your body as your outline and slowly start to waft the wand from your toes all the way up to the top of your head, along the sides, front and back of your body, almost as if you are drawing or tracing the outline of it.

If you want, you can cleanse each individual auric layer. To do this, waft the wand away from the body, remembering the seven individual layers. Brush the wand away from the body for a count of seven, moving it further away through each layer on each count. Alternatively, simply move the wand about 2.5cm (1in) away from your body, wafting or 'dusting' it in an outwards direction away from your body for a count of seven while visualising the smoke wafting its way through each auric layer. You could use your joints – ankles, knees (back and front) – and chakra points as landmarks along the body if you are nervous about missing an area and not covering your whole bodily/auric landscape!

Everyday Effects of the Now Age

I'd be lying to you if I didn't tell you that technology – your phone, your TV, your laptop – doesn't affect your aura. So do alcohol and diet have an impact on your energy rainbow. If you start to feel emotionally heavy when flicking through social media, a TV programme or a movie that has left you feeling cold, counterbalance this by getting outside, meditating or tapping into any of the exercises in this book that resonate with you. Check in on your energies and see what needs to be rebalanced or shifted. Take a visualisation shower, ground yourself or check in with your aura and your flow, and see what colour needs lifting or if there is any energy dust or soot that needs your enlightenment.

If tackling a food or an energy hangover, have an auric cleanse: look at what has been affected by your blowout or splurge and focus on rebalancing the physical layer, layer 1, of your aura. I guarantee when you start to work with your energies and your aura, you'll be more mindful because you'll be feeling much sweeter. Your energy will shift and align, enjoying the clarity!

Crystals to Help ...

Crystals vibrate and pulse just as we do. They have the ability to draw energy into our auras and also to draw out anything that no longer resonates with us. I like to think of crystals as energy lenses or filters. Should you wish to draw in more joy to your aura, carry a crystal such as jade or aventurine and allow it to up vibe your frequency on the move. For a more loving flow, find a crystal that denotes unconditional love to you, such as rose quartz, and it will diffuse a loving energy through your aura in your home or on your person.

To boost your auric layers and colours: if you have been looking at your auric layers and you have, for example, yellow sunshine fun light, but feel it's a little cloudy or would like it to be more vibrant, seek out a crystal you are drawn to with the colour tone you desire to vibe at. Just by meditating or sleeping with that crystal in your hand or under your pillow or carrying it with you, you are inviting that vibe in, that colour flow. Watch how your aura dances and changes over the next three to seven days! You can do this with any colour that you wish to add more of to your aura or draw into your vibe.

To protect from tech vibes: shungite is my go-to crystal and I keep it on my phone (especially at night time) as it intercepts the low-hanging vibes that cloud up my mental flow. I also use it when travelling and moving through airport scanners, for example.

To freshen your energies: deeply enriching black tourmaline grounds troublesome energy, much like when you do your grounding exercise. It is made even more powerful when coupled with smoky quartz; I call smoky quartz the vacuum cleaner of the crystal kingdom as it sweeps up anything in your aura or your home that is not serving you, while black tourmaline empties the hoover bag. Keep at home, on your desk or wherever you feel you expend a lot of energy, but also feel charged up by doing so!

For support: amazonite is a wonderful, soothing support and you can choose which vivid shade of this stone sings best to you, be that white, yellow, blueish green, green, pink, red or grey. Superb for dispelling, filtering and breaking down the energetical effects of any concerns or worries that may be lingering in your energy, your aura. It supports us energetically to heal physical and mental ailments, so if work is stressful or your relationship confusing or if you pulled a muscle in the gym, this crystal will work towards helping you deal with these internally.

To work against self-destruction: green aventurine is the human energy shield for those feel they have someone who is riding their energy. It also protects you from yourself – from those harsh thoughts, habits or patterns that have led you to self-destruct before. You can work with this crystal to help release and heal these patterns and their effects on your aura.

For grounding, stability and harmony: rainbow fluorite is a blend of some really powerful colours, much like you, and again like you, no two crystals are the same in shape, colour or texture. It is a highly protective crystal and a joy to work with to stabilise your aura and your energies – and to ground you and release any energy no longer serving you. It is a harmonising stone too, allowing your energies to work towards vibing at the pitch you desire to be or to become.

If You want to Explore Your Energy Further

Energy healing – whether in the form of auric, chakra and crystal cleanings – doesn't only have to be for when we feel heavy or when we need to shift and release energies from our aura and being. We may just wish to explore our energies further, to heighten the vibe, to bath longer in the magic. Or we may want the support of an energy expert to shift and cleanse our energies, so we can move into a lush meditative state under their guidance and 'see' and feel with more clarity, as we work towards trusting ourselves all the more.

Sometimes there are some types of dullness or clouds that we just cannot seem to shift, that we have carried with us for years or months on end – perhaps even lifetimes (past lives included!). We have almost 'set' our energy at this frequency and to change its vibe feels almost impossible. But you don't have to do any of this work alone: reach out and let someone with a different offering or deeper level of experience work with you!

The right therapist is the person who feels right to you, much as you might choose a hairdresser. You have to trust their vibe, but remember that you are becoming expert in sensing this now because by knowing your own vibe, you are subconsciously becoming better at knowing whether to trust another's! I have listed some practitioners and resources at the back of the book for you to flick your energy feels through.

When you lean into your aura you are committing to understanding your true beauty, your true potential, and your true worth.

My Last
Thoughts to
You ...

So now you have all this information and all this skill, what are you going to do with it? How are you going to take it forward into this Now Age of ours? Whichever path you choose, please do keep growing, evolving and developing your skill. Remember that your energy, your vibe and your aura can change daily, so you need to continue to build in your energy checks and top up your daily and weekly routines until these practices become your Now Age normal, just as you might cleanse your skin or wash your hair. Then, if and when life throws you, or someone else's vibe tickles you the wrong way, you will have more than enough strength in reserve and trust in your new-found abilities to come through these ups and downs and stay true to yourself.

You are all shades of changeable possibility and potential and, in reading this book, you are allowing yourself the most magical gift – to see yourself as a *whole* in every shade, every sensation and in loving kindness. You are learning not only to feel what that is, but becoming able to see it for yourself. In being able to see and feel your whole picture in all its technicolour glory, you are learning what you feel and truly look like on an auric level, as well as exploring the depths of yourself that you perhaps hadn't yet considered or thought of for a long time.

The effects of embracing your aura and this work are only ever positive. When you lean in to your aura and your energy, when you raise your vibes, you are starting to understand your true beauty, your true potential and your true worth. From that moment on, you will no longer accept or expect a vibe lower than that.

Your aura is a reflection of who and where you are. If you don't like where you are, remember that you can simply readjust your energy to a vibe or a frequency more in alignment with where you want to be. This can and will change your life, if you allow it!

A few PLEASEs now for you to take away ...

PLEASE take your time, be patient with yourself and your aura. Watch as your flow changes and happily touches all those who are wherever you go. Take note of the changes in your everyday life. Watch how you and the people around you feel – use your energy, your aura, to work for you.

PLEASE remember that you are not fixed. You are ever-changing, so be kind, loving, gentle and patient with yourself. Use your energy to work on you, for you and for those around you. What you give you get back, so please spend your energy wisely – it's a precious commodity!

PLEASE keep your aura and your energy clear and clean. Declutter and allow yourself to feel lighter and let the light flow into you. *Befriend* your aura and your energy, for in knowing your own vibe you are subconsciously becoming wiser when trusting another's.

Most important of all... PLEASE trust yourself. Practice makes perfect, so let yourself see, know, allow and believe. Lean back and let yourself radiate. Let yourself be, and be seen, as the most amazing beacon of rainbow light that you truly are, for you – you are a rainbow!

Further Reading

Reading is powerful tool and picking what feels good from a selection of reference points is super-important for helping yourself to grow and develop your own feels on all things energy/spiritual. Here are some of my favourite go-tos for you to consider ...

Yasmin Boland, *Moonology: Working with the Magic of Lunar Cycles* (Hay House, 2016).

A Course in Miracles (Foundation for Inner Peace, 2008).

Ram Dass, *Polishing the Mirror: How to Live from Your Spiritual Heart* (Sounds True Inc., 2014).

Dr Joe Dispenza, *Becoming Supernatural: How Common People Are Doing the Uncommon* (Hay House, 2019).

Kirsty Gallagher, *Lunar Living: Working with the magic of the moon cycles* (Yellow Kite, 2020)

Judy Hall, *The Crystal Bible* (Godsfield Press, 2009).

Louise L. Hay, *You Can Heal Your Life* (Hay House, 1984).

Esther and Jerry Hicks, *Ask and It is Given: Learning to Manifest Your Desires* (Hay House, 2004).

Emma Lucy Knowles, *The Power Of Crystal Healing: Change Your Energy and Live a High-Vibe Life* (Pop Press, 2018).

Laurey Simmons, *The Inner Beauty Bible* (Harper Thorsons, 2017).

Michael A. Singer, *The Surrender Experiment* (Yellow Kite, 2016)

Dr Brian Weiss, *Many Lives, Many Masters* (Piatkus, 1994).

Oprah Winfrey, *What I Know For Sure* (Macmillan, 2014).

Trusted Practitioners and Stockists

For more information about me, Emma Lucy, and where to find me, or to book a session, please visit me at: www.emmalucyknowles.com

To get social: @your_emmalucy

Energy work takes place in all shapes, forms and guises – just like us! Whether choosing a healer or a practice, remember that it's all about the feels, so please trust your vibes. Here are a few practitioners and stockists that I am beyond blessed to recommend to help you start your explorations:

Acupuncture

Cal Wansbrough
www.yogainthebigsmoke.co.uk

Ross J Barr Clinic
www.rossbarr.com

Sarah Braden
www.sarahbradden.com

Energy work

Alexandra Swann
www.alexandraswannreflexology.co.uk

Stephen Turoff
www.ministrymoe.org

Bamford has an amazing array of alternative

practitioners
www.bamford.com

Cloud Twelve
www.cloudtwelve.co.uk

Sophrology

**Dominique Antiglio,
BeSophro**
www.be-sophro.com

Sound healing

Aisha Carrington
www.aishacarrington.com

Athena Ko
on Instagram @thegonggirl

Lisa Pauley
www.lisapauley.co.uk

Briony Sound Smith
on Instagram
@brionysoundsmith

**Other online communities
and apps**

www.gaia.com
www.wellnessofficial.co

www.naturaltherapy
pages.com.au/energetic_
medicine/energy_healing

**Stockists for crystals,
cleansing tools and other
resources**

The Astrology Shop
www.londonastrology.com

The Colourful Dot
www.thecolourfuldot.com

Crystal Harmony Sisters
www.crystalharmonyuk.
co.uk

Get Lit Retreat
www.getlitretreat.com

**MoonMist™ Aura Spray and
Crystals**
www.paoloreflex.co.uk

Mysteries
www.mysteries.co.uk

The Power of Three
https://roxannefirst.com/
collections/the-power-of-3

Soulstice
www.soulsticelondon.com

Southwood Living
www.southwoodliving.
co.uk

Ume
www.ume-collection.co.uk

Other online stockists for crystals and cleansing tools for Europe, North America, Australia and New Zealand

www.thecolourfuldot.com/
www.goldirocks.co

www.holisticshop.co.uk/
www.shamanscrystal.co.uk/
www.wildeones.com

Etsy international stockists

www.etsy.com/uk/shop/
AURAMORE

www.etsy.com/uk/shop/
BlissCrystals

Acknowledgements

My thank yous will be endless – but I will try!

To my family, my special squad, the Knowles: AK, Jen the Hen, you are such rock-star parents, they don't really make many like you, and my sister Becks – I know with you lot by my side I can never really fail. Becks, another thank you x 1000 for your communication and connective magic: you are my sister and my best buddy and comms guru!

To my soul family, my pals – you know who you are by the way it feels when you are reading this (yes, it's you!) – if I haven't said it enough, thank you for supporting me in being me when I didn't really know how, and for your patience with me when I go full-beam radio silence into my work ...

To the Pop and Penguin team: Laura, thank you for blessing me with this magical project and to Sam, Muna and Sue, thank you for showing me just what we can do in such a short space of time – you are the actual best!

This book was written during a really interesting time for us all (March 2020 – I'll say no more) and I must thank all my clients new and long-standing who came to me in that time-you really allowed me to add a whole other level of shine into the practices within this book without even knowing it: this one's for you!

To my friends now in the skies and stars above us – The Big Man, Eric, Lily, Chris, Tom, Lady P, Big T and Lady Mary, Albard, the AAs and George – THANK YOU for showing me how, even when my mind wants to doubt why.

This book is dedicated to all of you rainbows – to those of you who invest in it and therefore invest in yourselves – I thank you for you being you and here's to now understanding why!

All my love and blessings to you xxx

Index

Notes

Notes

Rainbow Waves: the Structure of Your Aura

Time to take a birds eye view of the layers of you! The visual representation on the inside cover of this book is designed to show you the different layers to your aura. The shape shows the layers as if you are looking down on the inner rings of a tree trunk, or the ripple effect from throwing a pebble into the water – with you in the middle and your auric energy layers radiating out. Remember this is not to scale – you are a powerful mass of expansive light!

The colours of your aura are changeable - day to day, mood to mood, emotion to emotion, experience to experience. For ease, I have colour-coded this diagram based on the chakras that have most influence on that particular layer. Please remember that your layers may not be showing the colours detailed here as they change from day to day. The colours of the chakras that influence each layer are fixed, but the layers themselves are not.

There is also a fun visual exercise in this should you wish to explore it. By gazing at the image, you can send a boost of the chakra energy to each layer of your aura. Alternatively, you can use the image to gaze at as you breathe deep and relax into a meditative state. You can then watch as the colours in the image shift to show you the colour and power of each of your layers! Go have fun... PLAY!

YOUR AURIC LAYERS

Layer 1 – the Etheric Body or physical aura plane (our health)
ROOT CHAKRA – RED

Layer 2 – the Emotional Body or astral aura plane (our emotional library)
SACRAL CHAKRA – ORANGE

Layer 3 – the Mental Body or lower mental aura plane (our belief patterns)
SOLAR PLEXUS – YELLOW

Layer 4 – the Astral Body or higher mental aura plane (where our heart is)
HEART CHAKRA - GREEN

Layer 5 – the Etheric Template or spiritual aura plane (speaking out)
THROAT CHAKRA – BLUE

Layer 6 – the Celestial Body or intuitional aura plane (divining our dreams)
THIRD EYE – INDIGO/ROYAL BLUE

Layer 7 – the Causal Plane or absolute aura plane
CROWN CHAKRA – PURPLE

EMMA LUCY KNOWLES

Emma Lucy Knowles is an intuitive hands on healer,
clairvoyant and meditation teacher. She has worked with
crystals and energy for over 15 years, helping people and
souls from all over the world heal their pain, find joy and
achieve success. Follow @your_emmalucy on Instagram.

MORE NOW AGE ESSENTIALS

BALANCE YOUR AGNI: ESSENTIAL AYURVEDA
by Claire Paphitis

BE WILD BE FREE: ESSENTIAL SPIRIT ANIMALS
AND GUIDES
by Catherine Björksten

BLOOM & THRIVE: ESSENTIAL HEALING HERBS
& FLOWERS
by Brigit Anna McNeill

FIND YOUR FLOW: ESSENTIAL CHAKRAS
by Sushma Sagar

YOU ARE COSMIC CODE: ESSENTIAL
NUMEROLOGY
by Kaitlyn Kaerhart